Greg!

What a [...] *share history* [...] *our book bring* [...] *encouragement to love & cherish each other as long as you both shall live!*

much love,

Debi

Walter

Cherishing Us

365 Tips for a Healthy Marriage from The Romantic Vineyard

by

Tom and Debi Walter

Printed in the United States of America

First Printing: February 2018

ISBN

978-0-9793251-4-4

DEDICATED
to
Jesus Christ
It is for Him that marriages exist to reflect
Christ's love for the church to the
glory of God, the Father

TABLE OF CONTENTS

About Us

THE ROMANTIC VINEYARD website began in November 2008.

Our desire is to encourage and help marriages grow strong to last a lifetime. We have provided hundreds of healthy marriage tips each day on our Facebook page since then. We would like to make these available to you in a convenient book for your encouragement.

We have divided the book by seasons with photos from vineyards at various stages of growth.

Cultivating a strong marriage is much like cultivating a healthy vineyard. It takes hard work, patience and the right influences to produce quality fruit. We must work hard, exhibiting patience as God works in both of our hearts.

We pray this book will be one such influence, reminding you of the privilege it is to be married. It will be tempting to read ahead. Resist this urge. Read one a day as a thinking prompt. What would it look like in your life? How can you apply it in your married life? Take your time and allow each day's prompt to build up the last prompt.

We pray God's richest blessings on all who read and use this book through the years.

In Him,

Tom and Debi Walter

SPRING IN THE VINEYARD

SPRINGTIME is the time when the vine-grower must walk each row of the vines to inspect them. The condition of the fenceposts that support the guiding wires, as well as the condition of the wires that support the vines. They are on the lookout for rotting posts, rusting wires and loose growth. The posts and wires which exhibit wear must be replaced before the vine begins to put forth fruit.

In marriage, spring is the time when we look carefully at our relationship. How connected are we to each other? Is our foundation secure? Is it ready to bear the weight of the growth to come? Invest the time needed in this season. Delaying may find you ill-prepared for what's to come.

Bud Break is the term used in the vineyard when the first signs of Spring arrive. It is when the first leaves break out and usually occurs in March. This promises another year of growth – another year of harvest.

Did you know the first three leaves which appear on the vine are actually from the previous fall's harvest? The leaves and the tiny clusters of fruit are stored in the bud and stay dormant throughout the long cold winter. No matter how harsh the weather the leaves and fruit are safe.

The fourth leaf and beyond all grow as a result of photosynthesis –

the warmth of the sun allows the vine to produce its own growth. This all sounds so scientific, but what is true on the vine is true in life. Allowing the warmth of God's Truth to penetrate our weary vines will enable us to grow and mature.

Spring is a good time to assess the vineyard to see which vines are in need of attention and which vines are not. It is during this time when you can see how many clusters of grapes each vine will produce. The vine dresser decides if the grape clusters are too many for one vine to handle, and prunes accordingly.

Considering our marriages, this is also a good time of year to take stock of our bud break. How have your vines weathered the cold of conflict? Or the freezing temperatures of the flailing economy? These are difficult times, and our marriages are not immune to the effects. But we aren't left to ourselves; God has kept us safe within His care.

He is the Supreme vine dresser, and He is very attentive to every branch of our vine (our marriage). He knows us well, and He knows how much fruit will be harvested, even in the early stages of Spring. This is a time to celebrate the growth we see and take stock of the areas in which we are wasting energy. We must be willing to say *no* to those things which are inhibiting growth in our relationship. These could be financial, relational, or emotional. Don't insist on keeping things in your relationship that God is wanting removed.

If you have hobbies which are draining the life and time out of your marriage – stop. If you are so busy with others, children included, that you have no time or energy to give your spouse – stop. If you are neglecting time together due to financial pressures – stop. This is an area you cannot afford to neglect. Marriage is an investment that requires our constant attention. Failing to tend to it will guarantee a poor harvest, if any at all.

Why? Why all the effort to tend to our vineyard? When we said our vows, it wasn't just to each other; it was in the presence of God,

Himself. He not only heard your vows, He sealed them in Heaven and grafted two separate vines together as one.

No matter how many harvests your marriage has endured, God has not for one minute taken His eye off of you. He is watching for the fruit, and His is a fruit which will remain.

This is a bud break worth celebrating! Growth in our vineyard means God is still at work, and as long as He is...WE HAVE HOPE!

MARCH

1. Marriage goes through many seasons. Some are fun, some are hard and some are horrible, but they are all part of learning to love one another more than yourself. Only God can enable you to love in all these seasons. Simply ask for His help!

2. We will never graduate from the school of our spouse. If you know them well, you will score high when the tests come.

3. Multitasking and romancing your spouse doesn't go hand-in-hand. The only hand-in-hand involved would be an all-out tug of war. Let go of the multitasking and focus completely on your spouse. Only then will romance have room to grow.

4. Romance begins by thinking and planning your days with your spouse's highest good in mind.

5. Ask your spouse what they are dreaming about for the future. If they don't know, help them find out!

6. Communication is the heartbeat of your marriage. If it stops, so does the lifeblood of your relationship. TALK and LISTEN as if your life depends on it. It does!

7. Five words which should never be spoken in a healthy marriage are, "That's none of your business." The truth is, it all is if you are one flesh!

8. Say *Yes* more than you say *No* when it comes to helping your spouse. Make them your first priority.

9. *"What counts in making a happy marriage is not so much how compatible you are, but how you deal with incompatibility."*
   Leo Tolstoy

10. Do something out of the ordinary today to show your love to your spouse.

11. Love and treat your spouse the way you want be loved and treated.

12. Stay current on issues your spouse enjoys. This will enhance your conversation and go a long way in building your friendship.

13. Defer to your spouse as much as you are able. This is good for your marriage and good for your fight against selfishness.

14. Remember, it's not all about me. Taking my focus off of me and onto God helps me accomplish what He desires, not what I crave. This is a great foundation for a peaceful marriage and one which glorifies God.

15. Feeling anxious about an unresolved conflict? This is evidence you have not prayed enough. Leave it with the only One who can fix what burdens your heart today.

16. *"Do not be anxious about anything, but in everything by prayer and supplication with thanksgiving let your requests be made known to God."* Philippians 4:6 (ESV)

17. Be careful of attaching motives to action. Unless we ask, we don't know what motivated our spouse's choices!

18. Be an encouragement today. This means to give courage to your spouse.

19. *"Now faith is the assurance of things hoped for, the conviction of things not seen."* - Hebrews 11:1 (ESV) What things are you hoping for in your marriage that you have yet to see? Have faith in what God can do. He still works miracles!

20. The hardest times are often the best growing times in a marriage. Work through it - communicate honestly - joy follows the mourning!

21. Marriage vows before God aren't fickle - they're what help us stick together when our emotions falter.

22. Be honest, but kind!

23. Remember, you are ancestors to someone yet to come! The choices you make in your marriage will matter to them.

24. Take advantage of marriage conferences when they are available to you. You'll never know what your marriage missed and how it may have helped you where you are today!

25. Sometimes the greatest encouragement comes by using no words at all - expressing your love physically to your spouse can offer the best support!

26. It's important to say *I love you* every day! Even more important to show it by how you care for each other.

27. "*I Do*" should be our response to each other every day. It's how we do life together. "*Everything I do, I do it for you!*"

28. Be diligent in keeping your bedroom free from clutter and reminders of work. Wash those sheets, dim the lights and play soft music in the background. Watch how it calms your spirit when you walk in the door.

29. LAUGH together.

30. "*You have not because you ask not!*" What is it your marriage needs? Ask God to help, but it may not be the way you expected or the answer you hoped for.

31. "*God causes all things to work together for the good of those who love God and are called according to His purposes for them.*" Romans 8:28 This is a promise you can cling to!

March Cultivation Questions
Our Communication

1. We know exercise is good for a healthy heart. If communication is the heartbeat of marriage, what can you do to exercise your communication skills?

2. In what ways does your spouse communicate love to you?

3. In what specific ways has your communication improved this past month?

4. Ask your spouse how you can improve in your communication skills. Then, practice what they share.

Date Night Prompt
Coffee Shop Date

If you can't go out to a coffee shop, pick an area of your home with comfortable seating and a nice lamp for ambient lighting. If you don't have a place set up already, consider moving some furniture to a cozy corner for the date. Think coffee shop cozy!

Prepare a light snack and hot beverages using the best mugs you have.

When your date begins, tell your spouse to leave their cell phone in the other room. Tonight is a night to relax over a cup o' joe together and talk. You can talk about current events, dreams or whatever else stirs your fancy. You just can't talk about anything that will heat up the conversation. The only heat on this date should be in the cup or in your bedroom. You can even play a favorite board game like chess or checkers, found in most coffee shops.

Dig Deeper - If you want some good questions to get the conversation going, try our Date Night Questions...

From The Romantic Vineyard Blog

Date nights are great, but sometimes they lack good conversation. This is why we make a rule on such nights to not talk about the calendar, the kids, work, school, etc. Make your date night conversation about the two of you. Below are some questions to help get you started. Pick one or two ahead of time to ask when you're finally alone and able to think. Most of all... have fun!

- ▶ What do I do that makes you smile?

- ▶ What is your favorite time of day and why?

- ▶ What is something you think your mom and dad wished you would have done?

- ▶ What can I do to show you my love more effectively?

- ▶ Tell me your favorite part of my body and I'll tell you my favorite of yours!

- ▶ What was different about your family as a kid as compared to other families?

- ▶ What is your favorite romantic memory we've made together?

- ▶ What do you love most about our home?

- ▶ Where is your dream vacation if money weren't an issue?

- ▶ What do you remember about learning to drive?

- ▶ Who was your favorite teacher in school? Why?

- ▶ If our love had a theme song, what would it be?

- ▶ What is the worst movie you've ever seen?

- ▶ Of all the things I do, what do you appreciate the most?

- ▶ What truth do I preach better than I practice?

- ▶ When and/or where was the most memorable time we've made love?

▶ Can you recall visiting your parents' workplace and if so, describe it and how you felt when you went there?

▶ Do I tell you that I love you often enough? Too much?

▶ Tell me your most serious physical injury as a child.

▶ Do I respect and honor you around the children? How about around our friends/coworkers?

▶ What is your favorite memory of the two of us together before we were married? Second favorite?

▶ Do I ever joke about things you wish I wouldn't? Do I ever joke at times you think are inappropriate?

▶ Of all you've done in your life, what has made you feel the most proud?

▶ Is my way of doing things too structured? Too spontaneous? How?

▶ If money and time weren't an issue, what would you most like to do?

▶ Let's come up with 15 minutes a day for the two of us to talk without being interrupted. How can we achieve that?

▶ What is your greatest motivation for getting up every day and going to work?

▶ What things can you always count on me for? (Try to name 5)

▶ Think of all our married friends. What are some of the positive things you see in their marriages that you'd like to see in ours?

▶ What part of the Bible do you read most often? Why?

▶ Is there anything that you feel like we have a hard time discussing? Why do you think they're so difficult for us to talk about them?

▶ How can I pray for you?

▶ What is your favorite childhood memory?

▶ If you could have dinner with anyone in the world who would it be and why?

▶ What was the happiest moment of your life? The saddest?

▶ When did you first notice me? What was the attraction? Is attraction still important?

▶ Who has been the biggest influence on your life? What lessons did that person teach you?

▶ Have I ever done anything to take the wind out your sails?

▶ Who has been the kindest to you in your life?

▶ What is your earliest memory?

▶ Can you remember the way we felt when our children were born (thankful, in awe)? Do you still feel that way? If not, what would it take for us to feel that way about them more often?

▶ When I get angry with you and you ask for forgiveness, do you feel that I forgive you by my actions as well as by my words?

▶ Do you feel like you're harder on yourself when you make a mistake than you need to be? How?

▶ Am I harder on you when you make a mistake than I should be? How?

▶ What things do I do that make you feel loved?

▶ If you could do anything and know it would succeed, what would it be?

▶ Do you feel the freedom to tell me anything you're thinking about us? About me?

▶ Do you sometimes get the impression that I put conditions on my affection and love for you?

▶ Do you ever feel insecure about my love?

▶ Do you feel like we share the responsibility in our marriage or does one of us shoulder the burden of some areas more than they should (finances, sex, parenting, spiritual matters, household chores)? Are you comfortable with the way things are?

▶ What ways do you like me to touch you? (Not only sexual.)

▶ Name three things I do for you that helps brighten your day and make you feel rested.

▶ Do you consider me an optimist or a pessimist? How do you feel about that?

▶ Do we show our love and affection to one another enough around our kids?

▶ Do you feel like our marriage is a good example to the kids? Other marriages? In what ways? Are there things we could improve?

▶ What positive things have our kids added to our lives?

▶ What is your strongest area of leadership? Weakest?

▶ What has been the toughest experience of your life?

▶ What has been characteristic of your life when you have been "on fire" for God (or passionate)?

▶ As you look at your life this past six months, what area of growth are you most encouraged about?

▶ What has helped you grow in your walk with God this past year?

▶ Characterize your spiritual life this past year.

▶ What is one thing you've learned about God this past year?

▶ What is one thing you've learned about yourself this past year?

▶ What is one thing you've learned about me this past year?

▶ If you could relive one day of our married life which would it be and why?

► In what ways have you matured in the past year?

► If you could meet one person from history who would it be and why?

► In the past six months, what has been your most encouraging experience? Discouraging?

► What one aspect or thing in your life are you most encouraged about or thankful for right now?

► What is your most difficult pressure or challenge at present?

► What is your favorite romantic memory we've made together?

► What is a current source of stress?

► What have you been asking God for in prayer recently?

► What things are likely to cause you to cry? What has caused you to cry most recently?

► In what way would you like to grow in your walk with God this year?

► How am I doing in the area of romance?

► What do you see as the area of greatest strength in our marriage? Weakness?

► A quality I most admire in you is . . .

► How am I doing in communicating with you?

► A situation where I was especially proud of you was . . .

► Am I pursuing the closest relationship possible with you? How can I grow in that?

► What is your most difficult pressure or challenge at present?

► What is the area in which we most need to grow our relationship?

► How are we doing at building family identity and memories?

▶ What is your favorite time of the year? What memories do you most enjoy from then?

▶ What things did you see in me that made you want to marry me?

▶ What about our marriage makes you happy?

▶ What about our marriage makes you sad?

▶ What is the greatest strength/weakness of our marriage?

▶ Of our friends, whose marriage do you respect and why?

▶ What do you think God is doing in our marriage right now?

▶ What are you dreaming about right now?

▶ Where would you like us to be 10 years from now?

▶ How is your soul?

▶ What is the most courageous thing you've ever done?

APRIL

1. Be willing to do the hard work necessary to keep the lines of communication open at all times. "This is what I heard; is this what you meant?" Is a good question to ask often!

2. Purpose to look at your spouse when they're talking to you or others. This helps you listen and shows respect.

3. French kiss your spouse often! Ooh-la-la!

4. Think of all the things your spouse does RIGHT and praise them for it. Far too often we only see what is WRONG, and grumble about it. Praise cultivates the soil of the heart for seeds that will produce a lasting harvest.

5. You know you understand grace when you can give grace to those who don't think they need it.

6. Do not despise small beginnings. Any effort your spouse makes in the right direction should be encouraged!

7. When compliments are given to you from your spouse, the only proper response is, "Thank you!"

8. STOP, LOOK, and LISTEN! Realize your ears and eyes belong to your spouse. What you allow yourself to hear and see affects them as much as it does you, either for good or evil.

9. It is imperative that inhibitions are not permitted to inhibit your intimacy!

10. Take into account that a successful marriage requires falling in love many times, always with the same person.

11. Success in marriage does not come purely from finding the right person, but in being the right person.

12. Pretending things are okay when they're not only delays the inevitable confrontation. Be mature and talk it out; get help if need be! Your marriage is worth it!

13. Tell your spouse you love them without using words.

14. Don't wait for special occasions to write notes of affection...do it today and put it somewhere so they'll find it!

15. When feeling down and discouraged, talk to your spouse about everything concerning you using only personal pronouns like "I or me," instead of using pointing or accusing pronouns such as "you!"

16. *"Know this, my beloved brothers: let every person be quick to hear, slow to speak, slow to anger; for the anger of man does not produce the righteousness of God."* - James 1:20

17. Praise your spouse in public whenever you have the opportunity. What is one thing you are grateful to your spouse for today?

18. Worship God together!

19. "I Do" is a daily choice!

20. Resolve to do nothing you wouldn't want your spouse to see.

21. Regarding marriage, the question, "Is the glass half empty or half full?" reveals the optimist or the pessimist based on your answer. Maybe the more helpful question would be, "Are you thirsty for more?"

22. *"To get the full value of joy, you must have someone to divide it with."* - Mark Twain

23. Our marriage vows that sounded so romantically poetic when we said, "I Do," are actually difficult in the "worse, poorer and sickness" parts of life. Pray for God to help you in your weakness to keep your vows "until death do us part."

24. Traditions are a way of grounding love in familiarity and routine. When our children were young, we had a tradition of Saturday morning waffles or pancakes. What are yours?

25. Flirt with your spouse by texting or e-mailing something unexpected to them!

26. Knowledge speaks - wisdom listens!

27. Recycling the garbage in your community is a good thing - recycling the garbage in your marriage isn't!

28. If absence makes the heart grow fonder, then imagine what being present in your marriage will do!

29. A marriage may be made in heaven but the maintenance must be done on earth. See Ephesians 5:33.

30. We must choose to L-O-V-E, which means to Live Our Vows Every Day!

April Cultivation Questions
Our Commitment

1. If success in marriage comes by being the right person, what are you currently doing to become a better spouse?

2. How well do you communicate your commitment to your spouse? Not sure? Then ask!

3. In "Living Our Vows Every Day," how does this strengthen your commitment to your marriage? What is one vow you are needing to cling to in this season of your marriage?

4. Traditions are born when we commit to practice something. What traditions are most meaningful to you? Your spouse? What traditions would you like to begin?

Date Night Prompt
Celebrate Our Wedding Date

This month's date doesn't take a lot of planning, but it is sure to bring back many memories.

After dinner and once the kids are sound asleep, put on your comfy clothes and cuddle up on the couch to watch the DVD of the day your marriage began. Use the pause button as much as you want to stop and talk about what you were thinking at the time, and consider how far you've come since that moment. Enjoy reminiscing.

If you don't have a wedding video, you can look through your wedding photos to stir your memory.

As a bonus, play and dance to the song you chose for your first dance together. End the evening by taking communion together to recommit your marriage to God and each other.

From The Romantic Vineyard Blog

DO YOU WISH YOU COULD LEAVE?

If you answered *yes* to this question, I get it.

Marriage is hard work. But the problem isn't that marriage is too hard; the problem is we didn't fully understand what marriage entailed when we stood on the altar giving our vows. I have a feeling that if all pre-marriage counselors addressed this issue before the wedding, there would be fewer marriages and those that made it would succeed.

Our society has placed an unrealistic expectation of what lasting love looks like. It's not happily-ever-after... although it can be. It's not a bed of roses with sparkling champagne, although it may be from time to time.

Marriage is the joining of two different people for the purpose of our holiness, not necessarily our happiness.

Our pastor of 30 years begins his initial pre-marriage counseling session with the question, *"What will it take for you to quit the marriage?"* He's always met with shocked looks and almost an offense. This isn't what they expected, but they'll later learn that it was exactly what they needed. He has them consider questions like these:

► What if one of you has a debilitating injury and becomes completely dependent on your love and care? Would you want to quit?

► What if your spouse is unfaithful to you? Would you walk out the door?

► What if you have a child that has special needs and you realize it's a commitment to lifelong care? Would you leave?

► What if you find out your spouse is unable to have children?

These are a few of the hard questions he confronts them with to crack their rose-colored glasses. Only God knows what life holds for a newlywed couple, and most of them only see the "better" not the worse the future may hold.

Marriage is hard work, but when it endures by God's sustaining grace for His glory, it is a beautiful thing!

We pray that wherever you are on your marriage journey, you will stay committed until death parts you. If your marriage is in a good place, work hard to keep it growing in the same direction. If your marriage is in a rough spot, find the help you need to get past the trouble. If your marriage has been difficult from the beginning and you don't know where to begin, start with your own heart humbled before God, asking for His wisdom and mercy. God is in the business of restoring broken relationships. It's never too late to renew those vows, no matter how many years it's been since you spoke them.

MAY

1. Don't expect your husband/wife to be like your girl or guy friends. They think differently than you. When you see this fact as good, maturity will happen.

2. *"He that cannot forgive others, breaks the bridge over which he must pass himself; for every man has need to be forgiven."* - Unknown

3. We may become discouraged when we don't see immediate fruit; grace is patient and persistent!

4. Never take for granted the one who sleeps beside you!

5. How romantic is your master bedroom? Time to put some thought into making it more inviting.

6. We have a chance to make changes that will affect the quality of our love and the influence on our children.

7. A seed dies before it grows, so too a death must occur for a strong marriage to grow. What dies? We must die to self and live for the good of our spouse.

8. Does your spouse know how you're feeling today? Do they know what struggles you are facing? If they don't, make time to talk today. Part of the beauty of one flesh is carrying each other's burdens and not having to walk alone.

9. Think before you speak. If your thoughts are born from a heart that is worried or angry, it is likely your spouse will hear nagging. If your angry and worried thoughts are taken to the Lord in prayer, it is likely your spouse will hear faith calling to them through the storm.

10. In marriage, as in California... if you find a fault, don't build on it.

11. Romantic moments can be as simple as pausing to quietly marvel at God's creation together.

12. Healthy communication is a married couples' greatest weapon. Use it often and watch your relationship grow.

13. Boredom in marriage can reveal an area of needed change. Only those who are willing to face it instead of running will benefit from it.

14. It's the little things you do or don't do that have the biggest impact on your marriage.

15. Vowing to love each other when facing times where neither of you likes each other very much, or the circumstances you're currently facing, is evidence of God's grace and the certainty you'll make it through.

16. Yours is the hand I reach for when I need comfort, help, and support.

17. Express the following to your spouse: "I'm grateful for the way you demonstrate God's love in the way you love me."

18. God is a promise-keeper, and He enables us to keep ours. If you're struggling to be faithful, ask the Faithful God to help you. He will!

19. Timing is everything – for communication, surprises, physical intimacy, conflict resolution, encouragement... choose the right time to initiate any of these with your spouse for the greatest benefit.

20. Romance to marriage is like icing on a cake... you don't need it to make it work, but it sure is sweeter when you do. Not to mention it helps hold you together.

21. Music has the ability to communicate our heart in a way words alone can never do. Find a song that expresses your heart, and text the link to your spouse.

22. It is vital that honesty frames all our communication with our spouse. But it's even more important that our honesty is cloaked in kindness, caring for them as you care for yourself.

23. Believing your spouse includes accepting their compliments and letting them be an encouragement to you. Sadly, many of us–oftentimes women–don't agree with our husband's words of praise, so we disregard them as flattery. This is wrong. We should receive their words of encouragement with sincere thanks.

24. When your spouse is struggling with (fill in the blank), it is your privilege to help them see it from an eternal perspective. God is faithful no matter the struggle. Pray with faith on their behalf, and watch what God does.

25. It's more important to work on how you think about your spouse in secret than it is how you treat them in public. The first fuels the second; get your thoughts in line with Scripture (love, honor, respect, trust) and your actions will prove it.

26. Strong, lasting marriages don't get that way because "they found a good one!" No, they get there by making good choices for the betterment of their relationship, day after day, even when those choices require letting go of what one wants for the good of the other. Every choice you make reflects your conviction about your marriage.

27. A healthy marriage requires regular check-ups to be sure the temperature in your relationship isn't too hot or too cold. It should be just right!

28. A physically fit marriage consists of sexual intimacy that is honest, vulnerable and unselfish.

29. To watch us dance is to hear our hearts speak.

30. Date nights don't have to be elaborate, they just need to happen on a regular basis for your marriage to benefit from them. Take the challenge to plan one weekly for a month and see if it doesn't make a difference.

31. The photographs you have kept of you and your spouse represent years of God's faithfulness in your marriage. Thank Him today for the storehouse of pictures you are blessed to have.

May Cultivation Questions
Our Friendship

1. What was it that drew you to your spouse in the first place? Spend time thanking God for those attributes, then write a letter or tell your spouse about it.

2. What are the benefits of having your spouse as your best friend?

3. In what ways do you sacrifice your desires to bless your spouse? If you can't think of anything, pray and ask God to help you begin.

4. Who are your closest friends? What is it about them that makes them so?

Date Night Prompt
Building Marriage Friendships

The following date ideas can be done with a group of friends or adjusted to use on a date for just the two of you.

Select four dates to go on this month. They can all be with friends or divide it in half—two with friends and two alone.

Dig Deeper - Friendship is an attribute of healthy marriages. If you are needing practical help in this area, we encourage you to read the next pages together and discuss the changes you can make.

From The Romantic Vineyard Blog

Six Date Night Ideas to Build Marriage Friendships:

Most times when we think of a romantic evening, it's just for the two of us. But there are times when it is fun to invite your closest married friends over for a nice evening together. And if you don't really have close friends yet, we believe this will help you see how vital they can be for a healthy marriage.

Following are a few ideas of what you could do to plan a night everyone will remember long after you've all said, "Good night!"

Never underestimate the influence a well-planned evening can have on the couples who attend.

Evening #1
▶ **Host A Wine Tasting Party** – This is fun way to sample different wines you may never try on your own. The link provides a variety of different tastings from which to choose.

Evening #2
▶ **Start A Dinner Club** – Pick friends who enjoy cooking and start your own club. The rules can be made to suit your likes, but we enjoyed our Passport Dinner Club. Every two months we met choosing a country to celebrate. Each couple was assigned a course to bring and it had to be an authentic recipe from that country. It was a fun way to expand our culinary skills as couples, as well as our tastes.

Evening #3
▶ **Host A Downton Abby Dinner Party** – Have your guests come dressed up to the nines. Serve food that is authentic from the Edwardian Era. You can even charge a small fee to have a more elegant meal. For those who can afford it, you could even have the evening catered. How fun to have a formal dinner party for no reason other than to celebrate your marriages.

Evening #4

► **Host a 1940s Big Band Party** – Have your guest come dressed for a night of Swing Dancing and custom mixed cocktails. You could even have a signature drink competition. The drinks don't have to be alcoholic. The emphasis isn't on the drinking, but on the romantic atmosphere created, and the fun enjoyed.

Evening #5

► **Host a Movie Night** – Create a meal around a favorite movie and then enjoy watching it together as a group. Provide lots of fluffy pillows and throws for each couple to snuggle up together. You could even arrange to borrow a projection DVD player. Use a large white sheet hung on a back fence or screened porch. Set chairs up in twos and call it your very own drive-in theatre.

Evening #6

► **Host a Make-Your-Own-Pizza Competition** – Invite couples to bring their own toppings for the pizza they think will win. Then, provide the dough and sauces and let each couple create their masterpiece. Judge the pizzas on their shape, appearance and of course, taste. The winners don't have to help clean up the mess.

The idea of these parties is to encourage romance between husband and wife, and to share the joy of having married friends in the same season as you. You never know when one of those couples will become life-long friends. We have three couples we travel with, who we've known for most of our married life. In fact we just finished a fantastic weekend together–we called it our Land Cruise, since we were unable to pull off a cruise this year for various reasons. But we discovered that it's not so much about where we go or what we do as it is about who we're with.

Friendships can enrich your marriage in so many ways. How have you found this to be true? Have you ever planned similar parties for the sole purpose of being with your friends?

From The Romantic Vineyard Blog

Attributes of a Healthy Marriage Friendship

We have encountered far too many couples who. after years of marriage. have nothing in common. This is a dangerous place to be. We become vulnerable to the wiles of the enemy whispering, "Is this all there is?"

If you find yourself in this place it is not too late to make changes, but it won't be easy. Healthy marriages are never easy to build or maintain. It takes constant effort. Marriage is like one rowing on a fast-flowing stream. To stop rowing guarantees you will drift, going where you don't want to go. Don't do it!

It helps to remember where you started.

It may have been years ago, but it is worth the effort. Take out old photos of things you did and places you visited. Reminisce the good old days and allow your friendship to spark again.

Psalm 9:1 says: *"I will give thanks to the Lord with my whole heart; I will recount all of your wonderful deeds."*

Friends enjoy doing things together. Even if you have little in common, do the unselfish thing and take an interest in what your spouse enjoys.

Philippians 2:3-4 says: *"Do nothing from selfish ambition or conceit, but in humility count others more significant than yourselves. Let each of you look not only to his own interests, but also to the interests of others."*

A few years ago, I got to thinking about what our life would look like with grown children who no longer live with us. I knew Tom loved to play golf, and I had only ever played Putt-Putt–hardly the comparison. So I took golf lessons. My goal was to become good enough to keep up with him on the course without causing him dread when I asked to play. It took three years, but now we enjoy spending a day together doing something he loves. (A side note: I love golf now too, and I'm pretty good at it–so Tom says.) It's easy to excuse ourselves because that's just not who we are, but a healthy marriage requires us to consider our spouse's interest above our own. I know that has a sting to it, but better for us to put a sting on ourselves than to be stung by the pain of a drifting marriage.

What's the practical application to cultivating friendship in marriage?

▶ Study your spouse. Even if you are years away from having an "empty nest," keep up with what they love and find interesting.

▶ Cultivate your friendship. Friends are friends because they make a priority of being together.

▶ Find ways to laugh together. The Bible says laughter is good for the soul like a medicine.

▶ Make love often–this is the one aspect of your friendship that no one else can satisfy for your spouse. Connecting skin-to-skin goes a long way in building intimacy.

▶ Don't cultivate any other friendship more than you do that with your spouse. We all need friends of the same sex. They are gifts from God to us. It is important to talk with your husband about something before you mention it to your girlfriends. Make his friendship and advice the one you seek first.

▶ Husbands, this goes for you as well. Don't make your man-cave a higher priority than you do date nights with your spouse. The unspoken words communicated by doing so speaks volumes to her.

If I were to observe you and your spouse on a dinner date, would I see a couple who enjoy quality time together? I pray so.

Summer in the Vineyard

Summer is when vine-growers get to know their vines, in an up-close and personal way. This is when the quality and quantity of the fruit will be firmly established.

As vine-growers walk each row, they must look for an overabundance of fruit. If there is too much, it will reduce the quality of the grapes. Great care must be given to prune away the excess. This allows the fruit that remains to grow sweeter and stronger.

This is also the time when pests enjoy the vines. As a result, the fruit is in danger if the vinegrower doesn't guard the crop. Some farmers use herbicides, while others take a more natural approach, weeding and pest-picking by hand.

You may notice rose bushes at the end of each vine row. It has been shown that roses are subject to the same mildew as grapes. Mildew on roses is evident before it is on grapes, giving the vine-grower time to treat before the damage is done. Summer is no doubt a time when hard work is necessary if there is to be any fruit at all.

Our marriages face seasons where our time is limited. We take on too much, allowing our relationship to suffer from want of attention. Being aware of this danger will help us trim our calendar, making room for our marriage to thrive and grow.

JUNE

1. Erosion occurs little by little, until one day a huge chunk of road gives way, demanding serious, costly repairs. Consider the road called marriage; what daily struggles are attempting to erode your relationship? Do something about it today, or one day the damage will be severe and unavoidable.

2. In a vineyard this time of year, good grapes are removed from the vine to make room for producing the BEST grapes. Be willing to remove "good things" in your marriage that are preventing the BEST from growing.

3. Whatever you do, do it because it's the right thing to do, not because it makes you feel good. Convictions will stand and uphold you even when you are weak. Feelings are fickle, and crumble under pressure.

4. Next time you are tempted to demand your own way, let your spouse have their way... just because! It is good to say *no* to our own wants and cravings, for it helps us become less selfish and more like Christ. The harder it is to do this, the more reason you should!

5. The best question to ask your spouse who is struggling is, "How can I help you?" And then be faithful to do so.

6. Our marriage can be compared to a house; God is the foundation, our vows are the walls, our intimacy is the roof, and our shared interests the front door. Spend more time caring for the inside of the house, and the outside world will notice as we come and go.

7. Honoring your father and mother includes helping your spouse honor theirs.

8. Encouragement is to marriage what vitamins are to health. A great preventive, especially if given DAILY!

9. Take regular vacations from the routine to reconnect physically, mentally, and spiritually!

10. Work at discovering those things you both enjoy doing together. It may be that you have to defer to each other in the process.

11. Think of one thing you could do or say to encourage your spouse today.

12. Always have your nose in a good book on marriage. It is the one relationship needing constant care to grow and mature. What are you reading right now?

13. Make time to take time for alone time, then your time will be time well spent.

14. Make the most of every opportunity to encourage your spouse. This is like the rain on a dry and parched ground.

15. Know your spouse's favorites. Plan to give or do one of them this week as a way to bless them.

16. *"The way you see people is the way you treat them, and the way you treat them is what they become."* - Johann von Goethe

17. Never discuss with your friends anything you haven't already discussed with your spouse. This keeps your marriage relationship primary and your relationship with your friends secondary, as it should be.

18. Just as the ocean has high tides and low tides, our marriages ebb and flow. There is purpose and beauty in both, but one must step back to enjoy the view.

19. When we get to the end of our lives together, the house we had, the cars we drove, the things we possessed won't matter. What will matter is I had you, and you had me.

20. Unless you are intentionally working on growing your marriage, you are drifting apart. A canoe not being paddled always drifts downstream.

21. The question, *"Did I marry the right person?"* was answered when you said, *"I do!"* Marriage is a lifelong sentence that ends with a period, not a question mark.

22. Watch your thoughts, for they become words. Watch your words, for they become actions. Watch your actions, for they become habits. Watch your habits, for they become character. Watch your character, for it becomes your destiny.

23. The advice of a 97-year-old grandmother: *"Expect nothing! Take the word 'expect' out of your vocabulary. Then, everything nice in life [and marriage] will be a wonderful surprise, and you will never be disappointed!"*

24. Ask good questions to discover what your spouse is thinking. Don't assume you already know!

25. Keep yourself healthy and attractive for your spouse; it will make you feel better too!

26. Do you want your marriage to grow? Ask your spouse, "What one area in my life would you like to see me work on to change?" Listen first, without making excuses. Pray second, that God would help you be diligent in seeing yourself the way others do. And then get to work!

27. God's Word provides everything we need, including strength for our marriage when times are difficult. Pray for His guidance as you read and see what happens. Warning... you may not read what you are hoping for.

28. *"This is what I heard you say; is this what you meant?"* Ask this question often!

29. Be your spouse's biggest fan when things go right, and their biggest support when things go wrong.

30. Notes of encouragement given in good measure make for sweet music!

June Cultivation Questions
Our Encouragement

1. In what ways does your spouse encourage you to be a better you?

2. In what ways do you encourage your spouse to be a better person?

3. Ask some friends whose marriage you admire what their favorite marriage book is. Buy a copy and read it together.

4. What is your spouse currently facing that you can take to the Lord in prayer? Commit to pray daily and watch what God does.

Date Night Prompt
Remembering

Plan a night together to play *Romantic Scrabble*, recalling all the precious memories you share.

Begin an Encouragement Journal
Psalm 9 says, "I will give thanks to the Lord with my whole heart; I will recount all of your wonderful deeds." Take some time and recall all that the Lord has done for you in the past. Let this produce thanksgiving to God for what He was able to do then, and let this inform your future that God is good. Start a journal where you both list the things you can remember and if you can't remember, ask God to help you. He will. What a testimony this journal will be not only to you in the years ahead, but also to those who are coming up behind you. It will stand and proclaim what God has done when death has already parted you in this life.

From The Romantic Vineyard Blog

Scrabble Memories – An Old Game with a Romantic Twist!
Tonight we played a new version of Scrabble that we made up ourselves.
Here are the rules if you should choose to play:

- ▶ Take all the Scrabble letters and place them face up on the table.
- ▶ Light a couple of candles for ambiance.
- ▶ Place the letters of your last name on the center of the board – however you choose, as long as the center X is covered.

- ▶ Give each player the points scored with your last name. Remember the center X doubles the value of the word. Since you are one, it simply makes sense you both get the points scored by using your last name.
- ▶ Whoever is the oldest goes first. Make a word using whatever letters you want, providing they represent a romantic memory you both share AND it ties into your name.
- ▶ The next player goes using whatever letters he/she wants, as long as it is a romantic memory you both share.
- ▶ Keep score of the points as you go.
- ▶ The goal is to see if you can use all the letters–filling up the Scrabble board with lots of romantic memories.

When you are finished, take a photo of your board to capture this new memory of all the special memories you have made together.

From The Romantic Vineyard Blog

Four Encouragements for the Discouraged Marriage

Marriages can go through all sorts of ups and downs as the years pass. This is expected; it's shared in most wedding vows: *for better or worse, for richer or poorer, in sickness and in health.* Knowing this helps, but when your marriage is going through a down time, it's hard to find needed encouragement. If you're not on guard, you can find yourself looking for greener pastures.

This is why we want to provide four encouragements to those who are discouraged in their marriage. You probably know all these, but if you're the one who is discouraged, you most likely need a reminder.

Encouragement #1 – Hebrews 13 says, *"Let marriage be held in honor among all, and let the marriage bed be undefiled, for God will judge the sexually immoral and adulterous. Keep your life free from love of money, and be content with what you have, for he has said, "I will never leave you nor forsake you."* Contentment is often associated with the pleasant place, but here God is calling us to be content because He has promised He will never leave us or forsake us. He will walk with us through the discouraging times, helping us see the big picture, the eternal perspective of life. So if you are looking down, take some time to worship God for this truth. Put on your favorite worship CD. If you don't have one, may we recommend Matt Redman's *10,000 Reasons* album. One of our favorites is *Never Once.*

Encouragement #2 – Philippians 4:6-7 says, *"...do not be anxious about anything, but in everything by prayer and supplication with thanksgiving let your requests be made known to God. And the peace of God, which surpasses all understanding, will guard your hearts and your minds in Christ Jesus."* Oftentimes, when we're discouraged, we allow our emotions to dictate and inform our thoughts; that is the worst thing to do. Our emotions are not to be trusted, especially when we are being led into a downward spiral. How do we stop this runaway train? By crying out to God in desperate prayer. Let Him hear your heart. Let Him hear your fears. Let Him carry your unbelief, and He will listen. He loves it when, in our weakness, we seek His strength, for this gives Him the glory He deserves. God has promised that

He will give us peace when we do. If you have prayed and still lack peace... pray more. Pray until you feel the burden lift. The peace isn't dependent on our circumstances changing. It comes when we learn to trust God in this place of uncertainty. He is our strong tower, and He longs for us to run to Him. David knew how to do this well. Read *Psalm 4* for an example.

Encouragement #3 – Proverbs 24 says, *"By wisdom a house is built, and by understanding it is established; by knowledge the rooms are filled with all precious and pleasant riches. A wise man is full of strength, and a man of knowledge enhances his might, for by wise guidance you can wage your war, and in abundance of counselors there is victory."* Seek help. There are times in all marriages where you simply can't dig yourself out of the hole in which you find yourself. In times like these, we must humble ourselves and seek the help of others. You've heard the saying, *you can't see the forest for the trees*, well in marriage maybe you can't see the answer because the problem looms too large in front of you. If your spouse won't go with you for help, then we encourage you to go yourself. Change begins in your own heart, for it's the only one over whom you have control.

Encouragement #4 – Psalm 9 says, *"I will give thanks to the Lord with my whole heart; I will recount all of your wonderful deeds."* Take some time and recall all that the Lord has done for you in the past. Let this produce thanksgiving to God for what He was able to do then, and let this inform your future, that God is good. Start a journal where you both list the things you can remember, and if you can't remember, ask God to help you. He will. What a testimony this journal will be, not only to you in the years ahead, but also to those who are coming up behind. It will stand and proclaim what God has done when death has already parted you in this life.

What other ways can you think of to encourage those who are discouraged in their marriage?

JULY

1. Be mindful of choices you make today, for they will be the memories of tomorrow!

2. Avoid assumptions. Never form conclusions based on what you think they meant! Ask.

3. Sometimes it is best to overlook a matter. Sometimes it is best to bring up a matter. Asking God for the wisdom to choose is what really matters!

4. *"Do unto others [spouse] as you would have them do unto you."* - Matthew 7:12

5. Feeling weighed down? Set aside time to really talk about it with your spouse. They may not have an answer, but just having someone listen lightens the load.

6. TGIF makes us glad. We should also TGIFY! (Thank God I Found YOU!) May Fridays be a weekly reminder of the blessing your spouse is to you!

7. Think about the one physical attribute you love most about your spouse. When you are together tonight show your love without words.

8. In the busyness of life today, pause and think of your oneness. Busy schedules cannot diminish this truth: God has made you ONE. Plan to celebrate your oneness tonight!

9. To keep from being too introspective in your own marriage, do something to bless someone else's, like volunteer to babysit so they can have a night out.

10. One can go a month on one good encouragement but nagging halts progress!

11. Always be on the lookout for romantic ideas; they are everywhere, if you are paying attention.

12. Do something every day to let your spouse know they are the most important person in your life!

13. When there are no words, a reassuring hug is all you need! Sometimes it is better to put love into hugs, than to put it into words.

14. Make the most of every opportunity to esteem your spouse as more important than yourself.

15. Emotion doesn't fuel romance, conviction does. The emotions will follow as we purpose to romance our spouse.

16. Think of questions as little shovels to help you dig deeper into more meaningful conversation. Healthy marriages dig below the surface on a regular basis!

17. In the busyness of life, take time to enjoy quiet moments together.

18. Like a vineyard needs fertilizer and rich soil to produce quality fruit, so too, our marriages need rich biblical teaching to produce quality fruit. We must not only listen to the Truth but apply it to the soil of our hearts for lasting change!

19. Instead of buying your spouse a card from the store, take some time to write out a special letter. Carefully composed words mean so much more!

20. Imagine if you were in your spouse's place today. Pray for them as if you were. Seeing things from their perspective brings compassion and unity in marriage.

21. Silence "if only" in your mind. "If only he/she would do/say/be, then..." This is destructive to marital intimacy and is based in unreality!

22. To be in love is good. To be in love and perfectly transparent is as good as it gets.

23. Believe the BEST about your spouse.

24. Vitamins help keep our bodies healthy. We need them in our marriage as well: Vitamin E for Encouragement, Vitamin A for Affection, can you think of others?

25. Keep the fun alive. Send your spouse a love note via text using numbers instead of letters. E-mail them the code, if they aren't able to decipher it themselves. Hint: A-1, B-2, etc. Then, serve Alphabet cereal for breakfast tomorrow!

26. Reading propels great conversation. Always have your nose in a good book, then talk about it!

27. When you say "Yes" to something you are saying "No" to something else. Let your "Yes" answers be for those things that matter!

28. We love in the light of His love. Enjoy the sunshine today!

29. Let your criticism be private and your praise be public.

30. Draw from your spouse's strength. It is God's gift to you for your growth in godliness.

31. Never let a day go by when "I love you" is not spoken!

July Cultivation Questions
Our Intimacy

1. Intimacy invites your spouse "Into Me See." In what areas are you prone to holding back from being completely known? Ask the Lord to show you why, and for His help in sharing this with your spouse.

2. What are some of your spouse's greatest strengths? Take time to share what you have discovered as an encouragement to your spouse.

3. The thought, "if only he/she would do _____" is destructive to intimacy in marriage. Try flipping it on yourself. "If only I would change in this area, our marriage would be stronger." If you can't identify what yours would be, ask your spouse if they have any thoughts on it. This is intimacy in its rawest, most vulnerable form.

4. Identify one area where you and your spouse have experienced the most transparency. Talk about how this has helped you grow closer.

5. Make every effort to keep the Home Fires Burning. Read the post on the next page together and discuss it on your next date.

From The Romantic Vineyard Blog

Keeping the Home Fires Burning

Tom was two badges shy of becoming an Eagle Scout when he quit; a choice he regrets to this day, yet what he learned during his Boy Scout training is so valuable. I have benefited from his knowledge and skill in a variety of situations. The most important one he learned was to never panic. He is rock solid when it comes to emergencies and I am so grateful, since I tend to operate on the other side of the panic spectrum. He calms me and reassures me that things will be okay.

We were at our cabin last week when the temps dropped into the "let's build a fire" zone. It got me thinking about how building a fire relates to building intimacy in marriage.

I asked Tom if he had ever started a fire using flint rock. To my surprise he had. He went on to explain how it works…

I watched this video (*https://youtu.be/J48srwPrv0E*) of the whole fascinating process. Seven steps to build a successful fire from nothing more than a knife and flint rock.

If building such a fire works, how many steps does it take to build intimacy in marriage? I wish it were always this easy, but if given the right preparation it can be.

Anyone who has been married more than a few weeks knows that husbands and wives are completely different when it comes to intimacy. It is helpful to understand and appreciate the differences in order to build a lasting fire. Like the flint and the knife which are two completely different things yet when they each do their part, sparks ignite!

Many couples are surprised by the differences and spend much of their first year trying to figure out the how's and why's of it all. Some even try to change their spouse which never works. God created us different for a reason. It's the differences that make our marriage unique from all others.

We encourage you to spend some time talking over the differences you've discovered when you're both in the mood. Discuss how you might grow together towards intimacy rather than letting the cool winds of indifference snuff out your passion. Here are some good questions to get you started:

1. What does intimacy mean to you?
2. In what ways do I encourage our intimacy?
3. In what ways do I hinder it?
4. If I could focus on one area to improve in our relationship, what would you want it to be?
5. What do you love the most about us?
6. What in our marriage causes you to long for change? The thing that makes you say, "If only he/she would do 'this'?"

We've said it before and we'll say it again; for our marriage to continue growing in all areas, we must be intentional. Keeping the home fires burning is no different.

Is it time for you to stir the embers and add some fresh wood to get yours burning hot again?

Date Night Prompt
Creating Your Own Retreat

The bedroom is the one room in the house that should be your very own retreat. It should be free from reminders of all other responsibilities and relationships.

Plan this month to clean it of clutter and everything that keeps you from relaxing together:

1. Remove all clutter.

2. Remove all photos of anyone other than the two of you.

3. Remove all evidence of work, whether it's a computer or piles of laundry.

4. Add low lighting (candles, dimmer switches, etc.)

5. Add music

6. Add fragrance (linen spray and perfume)

7. Dust the furniture and vacuum thoroughly.

8. Plan an evening to retreat together as you enjoy being intimate.

9. Play the classic game of *Clue* with a Sexy Twist as a bonus.

From The Romantic Vineyard Blog

Clue Date Night with a Sexy Twist

We all love the classic game of *Clue* where each player tries to figure out whodunnit. But what if the whole game was given a twist into a game of #whereyougonnadoit, instead. Are you with me?

This date will take some planning, and it will require some money to buy some special colored lingerie or panties, but it will be worth it. You'll also need access to the whole house, so make plans for your children to be elsewhere for the evening.

Supplies:

► Clue game board

► Candles

► Soft music or mystery music of your choice

► One piece of lingerie in one of the following colors: Mustard, plum, scarlet, green, white and/or peacock. (Or one of each if you're able.)

► Six objects you would enjoy using for a romantic rendezvous. For instance, a blindfold, a feather, flavored lipgloss, ribbon, etc. Assign each object to a game piece: rope (ribbon), wrench (blindfold), knife (feather), candlestick (scented candle), pipe (massage oil), revolver (lipgloss). You can use these ideas or come up with your own.

Next, make cards for each room in your house to match the rooms on the Clue Board.

Here is what you could do:
- ▶ The Kitchen = Your Kitchen
- ▶ The Study = Your Bathroom Shower
- ▶ The Conservatory = The Backyard
- ▶ The Hall = The Hall
- ▶ The Dining Room = The Dining Room
- ▶ The Billiard Room = The Family Room
- ▶ The Lounge = The Master Bedroom
- ▶ The Library = The Office or Schoolroom
- ▶ The Ballroom = The Garage or make this a Wildcard – the winner's choice

Play the game using the normal rules and try to figure out who did it and with what weapon and in what room. This will determine where you and your sweetie will make a romantic memory on this night.

If you don't have enough rooms to use all of the clue rooms, then pick different parts of a room, like the living room sofa, the living room floor etc. It doesn't really matter how many rooms you have. Once you determine #whereyougonnadoit, you won't care one bit.

Tell your spouse that you want to help him/her "get a clue" about how much you love them. Then, ask them if they're game.

AUGUST

1. Honesty is the best policy!

2. *"In everything give thanks."* No matter what circumstances you're facing, continue to show gratitude to your spouse.

3. Keep a surprise in the works for your spouse; it adds fun and excitement, not to mention romance!

4. Check your gratefulness meter - are you more aware of blessings or difficulties? Gratefulness removes the rust of discontent!

5. Marriage is a beautiful dance with only One watching... the only One who matters! And it is for Him that we dance!

6. *"Laughter is an instant vacation."* - Milton Berle

7. The one thing a spouse regularly fails to do (like pick up towels, dirty clothes, etc..) is the very thing that would be missed if they were suddenly gone! May we not complain but give thanks in ALL things!

8. Be the change you wish to see in your marriage.

9. If we say we believe God is leading us, then we must accept this fact when we don't like what we are currently facing. Trusting in God includes trusting Him when He seems distant. The truth is, He is closer than you know!

10. When annoyed with something about your spouse, instead of thinking, "Why do they do that?!" Ask yourself, "Why does it bother me?"

11. Do you talk to your spouse on the cell phone while driving? Do you text them while driving? Do you check your e-mail while driving? STOP. Put your cellphone in the backseat to keep you from being tempted to look or pick up the phone. Don't let "till death do us part" happen while being careless.

12. Don't forget the importance of having fun in your marriage.

13. Considering the vastness of the stars in the sky together will help you remember how big God is. He is more than able to help you in whatever challenges you're facing in your marriage. Trust Him.

14. Ignoring a conflict may silence the conversation with your spouse, but not the conversation taking place in your thoughts. Do whatever is necessary to resolve conflicts quickly for the health of your marriage.

15. Thoughtfulness is what keeps the flames of romance burning and always warms the heart.

16. Be sure your spouse knows that if you had it to do all over again, you would still ask her, or you would still say *yes*!

17. Happy marriages begin when we marry the one we love. They endure when we love the one we married.

18. Don't underestimate the power of those three little words, I love you.

19. Unresolved conflict is as dangerous to marriage as a rocky cliff is to a ship at sea. Be aware and do all you can to avoid the danger.

20. Never forget the foundation for a healthy marriage is Christ alone.

21. Gratefulness looks at what you've been given. Ungratefulness looks at what you don't have. A healthy marriage grows when both hearts are grateful.

22. Why do you do the things you do in your marriage, and who do you do them for? The answer to this question makes a huge difference in the quality and success of your marriage.

23. It is a privilege to pray for your spouse. Take your concerns to the only One who can change their heart and/or your circumstances.

24. Sometimes planning a special romantic date is all your marriage needs to add the missing element of excitement to your relationship. Try it and see if it doesn't supercharge you both.

25. Ask yourself, "When was the last time I asked my spouse for forgiveness?" If I can't remember, I have most likely missed opportunities to grow and change.

26. Acknowledging our sin doesn't free us from it. Freedom comes only through confession and repentance, which is available to all who trust in Christ's finished work on the Cross.

27. Marriage vows shouldn't be taken lightly. They should be remembered and followed faithfully.

28. Laughter and sex are both great stress relievers; enjoying both at the same time is a memory.

29. It's not hard talking to your wife; all you have to do is listen.

30. Living in the past isn't good for your marriage, but remembering where God has brought you since you said *I do* is very good. Especially when you do it together.

31. Feelings don't determine the depth of your love, conviction does. Do you have a strong conviction that marriage is for a lifetime? Then, work at your marriage like you would your career. You'll reap the benefits, whether you feel it or not.

August Cultivation Questions
Our Gratefulness

1. In what ways could you invest in your marriage in the way you invest in your career? Talk about it.

2. Gratefulness is learned. How can you choose to be grateful today?

3. Every marriage has times where God moved in a mighty way changing you and making you more like Christ. What is one of those times in your marriage? Let this inform your current discouragement and fill you with faith that change is possible. In fact, it's a promise! *"And I am sure of this, that he who began a good work in you will bring it to completion at the day of Jesus Christ."* Philippians 1:6

4. What irritations are keeping you from showing gratefulness to your spouse? Ask God to help you overlook the irritation and embrace a grateful heart for the many things they do right.

Date Night Prompt Surprise!

Plan a surprise this month for your spouse. It can be as simple as their favorite meal or as elaborate as a weekend getaway. Let your budget dictate the degree to which you can bless your spouse.

Key - Make this a memory they will thank you for in the years to come.

Need ideas? Start by making a list of things your spouse loves, e.g. food, restaurants, movies, activities, etc. Once you have your list, pick one or more and build a date around it.

Here's one couple's story that will inspire you to think out of the box when it comes to surprises:

Great Idea for Less Than $12
You know I love to surprise my husband.

You know I love creative date ideas.

I happened upon this blog at the recommendation of a friend, and I can't tell you how much I love what was shared.

This is brilliant! Read it and be inspired!
https://theromanticvineyard.com/2017/02/13/great-valentines-idea-for-less-than-12/

From The Romantic Vineyard Blog

The Secret to Deepening Your Relationship

It's something with which most couples start off, but slowly over time neglect to the hurt of their relationship. Reclaiming this one practice is a secret to deepening your relationship and reclaiming what you've lost.

What is this secret? Expressing gratefulness to your spouse in all things. Think about it. When was the last time you thanked your spouse for the regular things they do to make your life easier?

Things like:

- ▶ doing the laundry
- ▶ making dinner
- ▶ grocery shopping
- ▶ working hard at their job
- ▶ providing encouragement when needed
- ▶ helping with the kids' homework and extra-curricular activities
- ▶ paying the bills

The list can go on and on of regular responsibilities your spouse takes care of that you may take for granted.

For as long as I can remember, Tom has thanked me for doing his laundry each week. In fact, I've grown used to his gratefulness. That's the flip side of neglect. We can grow used to hearing I love you's and thank you's to where we hardly notice when our spouse says it.

My hope is that we will purpose to express gratitude for the everyday ways our spouse works hard to make our family-life better, by what they do and say.

Gratefulness is the secret to deepening your relationship, and appreciation for a grateful spouse is a double blessing.

FALL IN THE VINEYARD

FALL is the most rewarding season in the vineyard because this is when the hard work pays off. It is crucial to know when it is the right time to pick the grapes by paying attention to sugar levels, acidity and tannin. Many onlookers expect the vineyard to look lush this time of year, but actually the opposite is true.

Vines receive limited watering, which requires them to work harder. The stress caused by the arid condition produces the sweetest fruit.

Many growers choose the quickest way to harvest using machines. Doing so allows a lot of unwanted moldy grapes, branches and pests to be processed with the fruit. Picking each vine by hand takes time and manual labor, but the results are worth it. Especially if the fruit is being used in the making of wine.

All marriages face times of stress and hardship. Some resolve to ignore the circumstances causing the stress. It might seem easier. But to those who are willing to work together, sweet fruit is sure to follow. This requires a resolve of both the husband and wife. They must be willing to get their hands dirty, so to speak, in order to produce fruit that remains.

SEPTEMBER

1. It's important to know when to hold on and when to let go. Hold on to the covenant you made before God. Let go of past offenses and hurtful disappointments. You married a sinner not a saint, and so did they...but the sinner has a Savior, which enables you both to hold on!

2. If there is something you don't like about your marriage, don't grumble or complain. Do what you need to do to make it better. Don't let another day pass where you settle for mediocrity. Start by praying; only God knows what is needed to bring about the change you desire.

3. A husband and wife are to complete one another, not compete with one another.

4. *"My grace is sufficient for you, for my power is made perfect in weakness."* 2 Corinthians. 12:9 (ESV) Rejoice in whatever you feel is weak in your relationship. God promises to perfect His power through it for His Glory and our good. Rest in the sufficiency of God's amazing grace today.

5. To encourage your spouse is to give them courage. Be their cheerleader and believe in them when they don't believe in themselves. Most importantly, pray for them. True courage is God-given.

6. Be spontaneous and do something out of the ordinary this weekend. After all if "spontaneity is the SPICE of life," then imagine what it can do for your marriage?

7. Let your focus be on giving rather than receiving and you will discover the Biblical purpose of marriage... the completing of each other. Each spouse makes up for what the other lacks, making oneness a God-glorifying reality.

8. Remember your spouse can't read your mind. If something is bothering you about what they did or didn't do... tell them. But in a non-confrontational way. Love gives the benefit of doubt.

9. Rolling the eyes can be a sign of a disrespectful heart. Change the heart and the eyes will follow!

10. Never, never, never use absolutes in conflict, except when you're talking about never using never or always.

11. Make it your aim to be the best spouse you can be. How? By dealing with the log in your own eye before going after the tiny speck in theirs.

12. Think of one way you have been changed for good as a result of your spouse's influence and care. Share it with them! "Showing honor to whom honor is due!"

13. Keep a short list of grievances and a long list of gratefulness! What are you most grateful for today?

14. No one should know you better than your spouse! Their help should be the first you seek when troubled, hurt or afraid.

15. *"And whatever you do, in word or deed, do everything in the name of the Lord Jesus, giving thanks to God the Father through him."* - Colossians 3:17 ESV. This is helpful to remember - whatever we do for our spouse's day-in and day-out we do for Christ! We serve Him best by serving others with a thankful heart.

16. Patiently enduring unavoidable hardship can oftentimes be our best means of support.

17. Romance in marriage should be like a simmering pot... always ready and waiting for passion to reignite the flames. What's the temperature of your marriage?

18. Compliment your spouse in a creative way!

19. It is more enjoyable (and beneficial) to rub your spouse the right way, instead of the wrong way!

20. Reflect often on how far you've come, be it one year or decades. No one shares history with you like your spouse. It is yours alone!

21. A healthy marriage isn't derailed by unexpected illness, but is willing to stoop where necessary to help the other get back on track.

22. Consider what you can do today to help your spouse with what they're currently facing.

23. Consider your spouse's viewpoint as if you were in their shoes. This is the beginning of understanding and will help bring quick resolution to any conflict!

24. Commitment to your marriage is the bridge over troubled water, and guarantees you make it safely across.

25. Romantic marriages don't just happen. It takes time, planning and energy to have the marriage of your dreams. A work that pays off for a lifetime!

26. Make an effort today to do something your spouse has been asking you to do for a long time. Make it extra fun by not telling them you're doing it. Let them discover the completed job themselves!

27. Strive to be content in the place God has you today. Strive to stop comparing your lot with others. This type of striving glorifies God and strengthens any marriage.

28. Make Sunday a day for your family to rest and play together. Some of the best memories are made when doing nothing together.

29. Be critical in judging yourself, and charitable in judging your spouse. Not the other way around!

30. Never make assumptions. And never base your response on those assumptions.

September Cultivation Questions
Our Giving of Grace

Grace is the ability to give to your spouse something they may not deserve. This is only possible when we remember what God, through Christ, has done for us.

1. What is one area in your marriage that is difficult for you to extend grace? Devote yourself to prayer asking God to give you His heart on the matter.

2. What tip this month was the most challenging?

3. What tip was the most encouraging?

4. In the same way that it is difficult to extend grace to your spouse in certain areas, realize that they have areas that are difficult for them to extend to you, as well. Talk about these specifically with the goal of dealing with the log in your own eye first.

Date Night Prompt
Laughter Is The Best Medicine

Spend an evening watching YouTube videos that are hilarious. It might be good to search for them before the date begins.

Watch ***Thou Shalt Laugh*** on Netflix. Watch reruns of your favorite comedy sitcoms.

From The Romantic Vineyard Blog

The Cause-and-Effect Marriage Covered with Grace

I didn't even know my need until I saw the effect it was having on my marriage. Something was wrong between us. We weren't connecting. We weren't communicating. We were at odds living our normal everyday life. On the outside everything moved forward as it always did, but on the inside a discontent was growing in my heart.

Have you ever been there? Thinking thoughts about your spouse, your marriage and your life that you know aren't for building up? I'd be surprised if you said NO. We all have temptations to be discontent. The Israelites displayed this over and over for us in the Old Testament. None of the good God did for them lasted long enough for them to really change. Given the next hardship, they were right back grumbling and complaining, and as a result they became a stench in God's nostrils.

But thanks be to God that was under the Old Law. If I had lived then, I would have been no different. We are blessed to live under the law of grace–amazing grace. And this grace provides a way of escape from the shackles of discontent that would destroy all I hold dear.

I felt like my heart was far away and that it would take a long process to bring it back to where it should be. I told Tom I desperately needed a date night where we could talk. So we planned it.

I never want to get used to the look on Tom's face when he hears what I've been thinking. It's a mixture of confusion, hurt and disappointment. And knowing that my words have caused those looks works like a healing salve on my heart that softens it for repentance.

My time to talk is finished, and it's Tom's turn to respond. After pulling away to the restroom–most likely to pray, he returned with love, compassion and what I needed most–wisdom.

Time after time in our marriage, we've encountered roadblocks like this one. Either I caused it, or Tom caused it, or extenuating circumstances caused it. Whatever the cause, the answer is always the same: Grace! We need to extend grace to each other in our times of need. We need to pray for our marriage for the wisdom that alone comes from God. He knows the timely word or analogy we need to hear to set our focus aright.

I'm grateful for that night and for the breakthrough God provided. It literally feels as if the monkey had been removed from my back, where he was whispering ugly things in my ear. The saddest part of it all is that I listened to him.

In his book *Grace-Filled Marriage*, Dr. Tim Kimmel explains:

Grace isn't blind. Nor is it without nerve endings. A call to a grace-filled marriage doesn't mean we ignore, trivialize, or excuse our spouse's unacceptable behavior. Grace doesn't mean we lose our voice when it comes to dealing head-on with things that are clearly out of line. And grace doesn't remove consequences. God's grace is offered to us, but it isn't realized if we're unwilling to receive it properly. We have to repent.

Let's purpose to seek a grace-filled marriage. One where we are our spouse's closest friend and confidant. Where we can talk about anything without it exploding into a war of words. Let's listen, pray and then speak with the words of God provides.

This is a grace-filled marriage, and what we want to embrace as long as we both shall live.

Oᴄᴛᴏʙᴇʀ

1. Choose to be grateful for the season in which your marriage is currently. Longing for the next season robs us of today's joys and blessings.

2. Surprise your spouse with a random act of kindness!

3. We asked a couple married 55 years what makes it work? Without hesitation she said, *"Realize life is a moving target and you constantly have to adjust to get it right!"* He said, *"Be honest!"*

4. *"Give thanks in all circumstances; for this is the will of God in Christ Jesus for you."* 1 Thessalonians 5:18 ESV

5. A cord of three is not easily broken - Strong marriages tethered to Christ will endure through the fiercest of storms. Not because of their strength, but because of Christ who binds them together.

6. It's not love that sustains our marriage, but marriage that sustains our love!

7. Today is the first day of the rest of your marriage. Make it the best!

8. We have two ears and one mouth; we should listen twice as much as we speak! Listen to your spouse before you form a conclusion as to what you will say next.

9. Look at your wedding ring. It is a constant reminder of the love you share!

10. *"Count your many blessings see what God has done!"*

11. Magnify your spouse's strength and minimize their weaknesses.

12. Love bears all things. We express love to our spouse when we bear with them in hardship and weakness.

13. Praying with your spouse opens a window to your heart like nothing else. It is here where your spouse can listen carefully to learn what inspires, excites and frightens you all at once. Prayer encourages intimacy not only with God, but in marriage as well! Pray on...

14. Just like our bodies, when we discover sickness (problems) we should get the help we need. Putting it off doesn't make the trouble go away, it only worsens doing more damage! If a car is coasting, it is going downhill!

15. Complaining breeds discontentment!

16. Prove your love by not having to prove you are right!

17. Hearing your spouse pray opens a window into their soul and vice versa. Take advantage of every opportunity to open the windows to experience a deeper intimacy as husband and wife.

18. Consider what fruit will grow as a result of the seeds you're sowing in your marriage today.

19. What's the one thing you appreciate most about your spouse on THIS day? Tell them in an unexpected way...like texting, Facebook, e-mail, cookies, hidden note...be creative! Oh, and do it right this minute, or you will most likely forget!

20. As often as possible, go to bed together. It is a blessing which should never be taken for granted.

21. *"If you would be loved, love and be lovable."* - Benjamin Franklin

22. Failing marriages can be revived by forgiveness; healthy marriages are sustained by it.

23. Wherever you are, there you are. Be present, not distant.

24. Take a moment over the weekend to ask your spouse, "What do I do that makes you feel loved?" You may be surprised at their answers.

25. Gratefulness breeds contentment.

26. Outdo each other in showing kindness! Let the competition begin...

27. Guard what you think of your spouse each day - keep the fire of affection ablaze by charitable thoughts, not hurtful judgments.

28. Love is patient - practice this truth today towards the love of your life!

29. Praying together promotes intimacy with each other and God. Do not neglect this in marriage - it is what anchors your soul to what matters most.

30. Remember God's sovereignty when you're tempted to be discouraged about plans that didn't go as expected.

31. Do you have a pet name for your spouse? This is romantic and helps keep your love new each day. To make it more special - keep it a secret between the two of you!

October Contemplation Questions
Our Spiritual Unity

1. How often do you pray together? If not often, talk about why.

2. If your spouse is facing hardship, ask if you can pray for them before you go to sleep. Hearing your heart for what concerns them speaks volumes of your care of love.

3. What is one area causing you the most disappointment? Ask your spouse to pray with you taking your disappointment to the Throne of Grace for the mercy and help you need.

4. Read the same devotional, either together or separately. Doing so allows you to discuss what the Holy Spirit is revealing to you in Scripture.

Date Night Prompt
Treasure Hunts

Bookstore Treasure Hunt
Go to your local bookstore or library. Spend an hour or two looking at Christian devotional books. Purchase the one you both like best and start a daily habit of reading to each other before you go to sleep at night. This will allow you to both lay your head down in peace.

10.5.1 Mall Date - Fall In Love At The Mall

Plan an evening out together where you go to the mall with a different mindset.

This time you're not picking up your son's next pair of jeans that he'll only outgrow in a month. You're not buying Christmas gifts in a last minute frenzy or rushing to get in on that great sale which ends tonight at closing.

No, this time at the mall is to rekindle the romantic side of your relationship.

Here's the idea:

10 – Each of you are given $10 to spend on something or several things that will make your spouse smile. You can't go over $10 and any money left over can only be change.

5 – You also must take 5 pictures with your camera or phone along the way that communicates a romantic message to your spouse.

It could be the sign in a store window, the cover of a book, or the message on someone's t-shirt. It could be a picture of an object that communicates how your love makes you feel – like an elevator says, "You pick me up when I'm down!" You get the idea.

1 – Give yourselves each 1 hour to shop and decide on your meeting place afterwards. It could be for dinner at a restaurant in the mall or in the Food Court, or it could be at a coffee shop for dessert and coffee. Wherever you meet, make sure you have a place to yourselves to enjoy sharing your finds with each other.

At the end of the hour, meet and take turns showing your five pictures and then, exchange the gift(s) you purchased and see if you make each other smile. If you do–you win. If you both smile, then you both win! A win-win date night all around.

Dig Deeper - Sometimes we need to be reminded of what's of most importance. Take some time and read the next pages together. We are quite certain you'll have a lot to discuss when you are finished.

From The Romantic Vineyard Blog

A Soul Filled with God

Gary Thomas has written a devotional book for couples titled, *Devotions for a Sacred Marriage*. Today we want to share with you one devotion that has had a profound effect on us. The amazing thing is – this is what we have experienced in our own marriage and what fuels our desire to help others cross over into a relationship that gives, instead of expects to receive. This is work God desires to do! We pray you'll find some time to talk about it and implement changes as needed.

A Soul Filled with God
from Devotions for a Sacred Marriage
by Gary Thomas
(Used with Permission)

One thing I ask of the Lord, this is what I seek: that I may dwell in the house of the LORD all the days of my life, to gaze upon the beauty of the LORD and to seek him in his temple." Psalm 27:4

Personal worship is an absolute necessity for a strong marriage. It comes down to this: If I stop receiving from God, I start demanding from others. Instead of appreciating and loving and serving others, I become disappointed in them. Instead of cherishing my wife, I become aware of her shortcomings. I take out my frustrations with a less-than-perfect life and somehow blame her for my lack of fulfillment.

But when my heart gets filled with God's love and acceptance, I'm set free to love instead of worrying about being loved. I'm motivated to serve instead of becoming obsessed about whether I'm being served. I'm moved to cherish instead of feeling unappreciated.

Madeleine complains about a lack of spiritual intimacy in her relationship with her husband, Martin. "He's never been what you might call her a spiritual leader," she says, and this has become almost an obsession for her – as though her own spiritual health depends on her husband suddenly becoming mature.

"Did Teresa of Avila have a spiritual leader?" I asked her. "Madame Guyon? Mother Teresa of Calcutta? What about the countless widows who now pursue God on their own? Were – and are – their lives empty simply because they aren't married to a spiritually mature man?"

Tim is upset because his wife never initiates physical intimacy. Like Madeleine, he's become fixated on one issue in his marriage, so that he can hardly even pray – which makes him feel more emotionally dependent on the sexual intimacy he's not getting. "Tim," I said, "I remember praying with a husband whose wife was in the last stages of severe multiple sclerosis. It had been years since they could enjoy anything even approximating normal sexual relations. Do you think God has wired this world in such a way that her husband has no chance to be happy and fulfilled because his wife can't initiate – or even perform?"

Tim had expected me to preach only to his wife, not to him. "In fact," I added, "he found great joy in taking care of her – and that meant cleaning out a bedpan on a regular basis."

Certainly, spiritual intimacy and sexual relations are legitimate desires, but you know what? Whenever I place my happiness in the hands of another human being, I'm virtually guaranteeing some degree of disappointment. It can be as frivolous as a barista not getting my chai at Starbucks just the way I like it, or it can be as profound as some pastor I really admire falling into sin.

That's why worship sets me free. It meets my most basic need – to rest in the fact that I am known and loved, that I have a purpose, and that my eternal destiny and delight are secure – so that lesser needs (including spiritual companionship and sexual desires) serve the role of an occasional dessert rather than my main meal.

It's simply not fair to ask your spouse to fulfill you. No one can. If you expect your spouse to be God for you, your spouse will fail every day and on every account. Not only that, should your disappointment lead you to divorce, your second, third, and even fourth spouses will fail you too!

Only one can love you like God, with a perfect, constantly steady, and giving love – and that is God himself. When the "one thing" we seek is to dwell in God's house, to gaze upon his beauty, and to seek him in his temple, our soul's sense of desperate need is met in our heavenly Father's arms. Then we leave this temple and find tremendous joy in giving, in loving, and in serving rather than in keeping close accounts as to whether we're being loved or being served.

Maybe it's just me, but I've seen a constant formula at work in my life: the less I receive from God, the more I demand from my wife; the more I receive from God, the more I am set free to give to my wife.

The best thing you can do for you for your marriage is to fill your soul with God. Start defining disappointment with your spouse as spiritual hunger, a cosmic call to worship. Marriage is a wonderful institution, but it is limited. It can't replace God. Don't ask it to.

NOVEMBER

1. *"In marriage, to be meek is not to be weak or vulnerable, but to be so committed to your spouse that you will sacrifice for his/her good. A meek person sees the futility of responding to sin with sin."* - Dave Harvey

2. Make it easy for your spouse to love you by preferring them over your own wants and desires.

3. What is the marriage of your dreams? Do something today to help your dreams come true.

4. It is important to think well of your spouse, for then you will speak well of them to others.

5. Marriage is a seed which when planted begins to grow. Only God knows the fruit which will be produced in the years ahead. Storms will come. Heat will rise. Leaves will fall, and droughts will linger. How deep the roots grow will make all the difference in the endurance of the tree. Let your roots grow deep in love for God. He is your rock and foundation.

6. Sometimes necessary words can be painful words, but they should never be hurtful words. Choose your words carefully, but don't neglect them either. *"Faithful are the wounds of a friend."* Proverbs 27:6 ESV

7. Kindness is one of the best gifts you can give your spouse. Treating them this way softens the heart to endure hardship together.

8. Marriage is a promise to learn how to live and grow together for the rest of your life.

9. Experiencing God's beauty in creation together inspires the appreciation of the beauty found in your marriage. Both are awe-inspiring and worthy of praise to God.

10. If your marriage had a soundtrack, what song would be playing today?

11. Be present when you are spending time with your spouse. It's easy to ignore them when you aren't paying attention, and ignoring is a subtle way of saying you really don't care. Put the gadgets down and give your spouse your best attention. It will go a long way in promoting intimacy in your marriage.

12. Don't forget the importance of having fun in your marriage. Lighten up. Do something silly. Make your spouse laugh. It will do wonders for the health of your relationship.

13. God is the God of the storm. He alone knows what you need to bring your marriage safely through the storms you face. Run to Him and allow Him to be your shelter and your guide. He will protect you and help you as no one else can.

14. Never tire of marveling at the intricate way God has ordained for your life to fit perfectly with your spouse.

15. Spiritual intimacy in marriage shows empathy for others through prayer.

16. Work on your relationship when things are going well, so your foundation is strong when the winds of adversity blow.

17. There is key that helps unlock the beauty of new seasons–Communication! Use it often to keep barriers from holding you back.

18. On the next full moon – reflect on the fruit you're currently harvesting in your marriage and give thanks.

19. Celebrate your spouse's big moments as if they were your own.

20. Vow to pray for your spouse lifting their concerns before the Father because you love them.

21. Praying for your spouse is a privilege that should not be neglected. Give your spouse your heart of prayer and watch God's heart of love respond to your request.

22. Reflect on the history you share with your spouse today. It is a bridge that connects the past to the future.

23. Communication is the heartbeat of a marriage. Measure your pulse by asking good questions and don't ignore the blocks you find. It could mean a slow death is taking place.

24. God's beauty in creation is a reminder of the beauty He intends for us to display in our marriage.

25. Do all you can to help your spouse's dreams come true.

26. Being faithful in the little things has a big impact on the growth of your marriage.

27. Remember, intimacy is nurtured behind closed doors.

28. It's important to remember in marriage, if you're not rowing, you are drifting.

29. Pray this often: "Father, make us aware of reality, and give us courage to address those pressures that would destroy our marriage, family and legacy."

30. *"True humility does not know that it is humble. If it did, it would be proud from the contemplation of so fine a virtue."* Martin Luther

November Cultivation Questions
Our Humility

1. In what ways has your spouse put your needs above their own? In what ways have you put their needs above your own? Share your thoughts with each other.

2. Humility is not thinking less of yourself but thinking of yourself less. What is one way you could practice this in your marriage?

3. Is there an issue that keeps occurring without resolve in your marriage? Consider how pride might be keeping you from deferring to your spouse in the matter. This is not easy to do—admitting your fault—but doing this is what takes your marriage from mediocre to great.

4. Consider your spouse's perspective; How easy do you make it to be married to you? Honesty is the first step towards humility.

Date Night Prompt Discovery

Make this the night you discover more about how your spouse thinks. Take the **Five Love Languages** test (link below) to see what speaks love the most to each other. Even if you have taken this test before, do it again. As the years pass, our preferences change, too.

The Five Love Languages are:

- Words of Affirmation
- Quality Time
- Receiving Gifts
- Acts of Service
- Physical Touch

Once you complete the test, talk about how the results play out in your marriage relationship. What can you do to improve? What are you doing right?

http://www.5lovelanguages.com/profile/

Winter in the Vineyard

One would think this season of the year is a time of rest in the vineyard, but you would be wrong. Winter is the time when trimming of the vines is needed. If it is done during late fall, the vines risk putting out new growth. If it is done in early spring, it will damage the tender bud breaks. Timing and placement of the trims are essential for a healthy crop. It is also important to keep enough of the branches so there isn't too much gap between the vines.

What a great metaphor for marriage. When things slow down in our lives, it is important to make the most of this time. We must focus on areas of our relationship that need trimming. It could be physical clutter in the home, or emotional clutter of things in need of communication. But make sure you don't cut yourself off from others who can come alongside to help you resolve these issues.

Doing so encourages healthy new growth in the springtime resulting in more fruit for God's glory!

1 Photo by Cynthia Bennet, Sogn Valley Vineyard, used with permission.

DECEMBER

1. Choose to listen to the wants, needs and feelings of your spouse.

2. Never underestimate the power of the Gospel to change your marriage. The Bible says that nothing is impossible with God. If He can raise the dead, He can certainly rekindle the romance in your marriage.

3. *"The three qualifications of a good surgeon are requisite in a reprover: He should have an eagle's eye, a lion's heart, and a lady's hand; in short, he should be ensued with wisdom, courage, and meekness."* - Matthew Henry

4. When you are worried, anxious and troubled about your marriage, this simply is your heart's alarm system calling you to prayer. "Let your requests be made known to God and the peace of God will guard your heart..."

5. Say a quick prayer and have the conversation you've been avoiding. This is acting on your wedding vows - for better or worse.

6. Make it your pledge to never keep something secret from your spouse.

7. There is no greater gift you can give your spouse than forgiveness when they ask for it.

8. Kiss often... and enjoy it!

9. Sometimes the best thing to say is...nothing. Sometimes the best thing to say is...please forgive me. Sometimes the best thing to say is... tell me what is on your heart? It takes wisdom to choose what is best in the moment. Pray for wisdom!

10. Dennis Rainey on the empty nest stage: "*Every room, every corner of the house, every nick in the coffee table will be crowded with memories.*" And Barbara and I will "*sit quietly by the fire and listen to the laughter in the walls.*"

11. You can tell how strong a person is by what it takes to discourage them.

12. Turn critical complaints into faith-filled prayers and watch what God will do.

13. *"Teach us to number our days that we might get a heart of wisdom."* - Psalm 90:12. Moses wrote this psalm right after the Israelites cowered in fear about the Promised Land. God sent them back into the wilderness for 40 years! In the face of a bad report, pray for wisdom from God instead of reacting in fear.

14. What is weighing on your spouse's heart today? Don't know? Ask. If you do know, spend some extended time praying for them!

15. Be accountable. Seek friends who will speak the Truth to you to help you become a better spouse!

16. Help your spouse reach their goals one day, one decision at a time. Our goal for today? Organize our filing system... the hum of a shredder makes me happy!

17. Nothing will strengthen your marriage more than cultivating a sincere love for God.

18. Silence the critic within towards your spouse.

19. When you pray for your spouse - believe God not only hears you, but chooses to answer. Pray every day for the one with whom you are closest in this life!

20. *"Husbands live with your wives in an understanding way."* 1 Peter 3:7a ESV.

21. If money is tight this year, and you are unable to exchange gifts to each other, why not write a special letter telling your spouse all the ways they are a "gift" to you? Wrap it in a small box, then a little larger box, and wrap it all up to give them on Christmas Eve. Or you could wrap yourself up for them to *unwrap.* Such gifts are much better than those which are store bought!

22. As in prayer, so in marriage, it's better to have a heart without words, than words without a heart!

23. Remember you're on the same team and you fight a common enemy! It's important to not lose sight of this fact when you are in a conflict.

24. *"The test of good manners is to be patient with bad ones."* – Gabirol

25. The day after a holiday can be stressful - pray for your spouse right now for help in all they're facing.

26. Pursue God with all your heart and see if it doesn't make all the difference in your marriage!

27. Honor your spouse by treating them with respect and kindness. It should be obvious to others that you respect each other by observing how you talk and look at one another.

28. Speaking with a couple celebrating their 50th wedding anniversary...We asked their advice for a long, happy marriage. He said, *"Two words--Yes, Dear!"* She said, *"After one year I was ready to leave, and my Mom said, if you do you'll immediately start looking for a new husband; better to keep the one you've got and make it work!"*

29. Always make yourself available to your spouse and their requests - for talking, errands, household chores and SEX! Procrastination exasperates your spouse!

30. Listening to what your spouse isn't saying is often the most urgent to discuss. The healthy marriage draws from the deep well of understanding, providing words when there are none.

31. Celebrate the New Year with a lingering kiss and then...

December Cultivation Questions
Our Honesty

1. Do you have secret struggles of which your spouse is unaware? Why? The humble seek the advice and help of their spouse because of their unwavering commitment to the good of the marriage. Secrets block intimacy. Honesty invites it in.

2. Realize that being honest is not a license to say whatever is on our mind to say. "I was just being honest" following hurtful words isn't love, it's selfish manipulation. Choose your words with kindness as you would want to hear them spoken to you.

3. Ask each other—In what ways do I make it easy for you to be honest with me?

4. In what ways do I make it difficult to be honest? This is a time to listen and not react to what you hear.

Date Night Prompt
Favorite Things

Plan a date of all your spouse's favorite things. It can be at home or out on the town. It can be local or a weekend away. Whatever you are able to do, make it the best of the best in your spouse's opinion.

From The Romantic Vineyard Blog

Honesty Breeds Intimacy

There have been two MAJOR times in our marriage when honesty – the painful kind of honesty you know is going to hurt your spouse – is necessary. The first happened during our third year of marriage when I was pregnant with our first baby. We were out to dinner (which deciding where to eat became a major conflict all in itself), looking over the menu across from each other in a dimly lit room. Suddenly, I had a question I knew I needed to ask Tom. It was one of those probing questions into the heart.

When I asked, Tom's countenance immediately changed. He looked like he had been caught stealing; being dishonest about something or hiding something from your spouse is a lot like stealing. He began to confess to me several things I would have never suspected or imagined.

This was the moment God used to give us an open door to deeper intimacy. Although, after hearing all he had to say – intimacy was the LAST thing on my mind. I was hurt. I was angry. And I was shocked. How could I not have known?

Once everything was out in the open, our talks became more serious, sober. No longer were we seeing life through rose-colored glasses, those had been smashed. But we now had a deeper focus on the beauty of grace. Unmerited grace. Grace that is capable of forgiving and helping us move forward.

This was the beginning of our hearts being knit together with a love that comes from God. It is holy – unnatural. He who has forgiven us much enabled me to forgive Tom much. As the years passed we realized how pivotal this night was in solidifying our relationship. Our love was stronger and deeper because God helped us be brutally honest.

Fast-forward to our 18th year of marriage when it was my turn to feel the heat. I had been reading Andrew Murray's book, *Humility*, and as I came to the end I felt prompted by the Lord to take his 30-day challenge. It is called *A Prayer For Humility*. He says:

> *Here I will give you an infallible touchstone that will tie all to the*

113

truth. It is this; retire from the world and all conversation, only for one month. Neither write, nor read, nor debate anything with yourself. Stop all the former workings of your heart and mind. And, with all the strength of your heart, stand all this month, as continually as you can, in the following form of prayer to God. Offer it frequently on your knees. But whether sitting, walking, or standing, be always inwardly longing and earnestly praying this one prayer to God:

"That of His great goodness He would make known to you, and take from your heart, every kind and form and degree of pride, whether it be from evil spirits, or your own corrupt nature; and that He would awaken in you the deepest depth and truth of that humility which can make you capable of His light and Holy Spirit."

Reject every thought, but that of waiting and praying in this matter from the bottom of your heart, with such truth and earnestness as people in torment wish to pray and be delivered from it. If you can and will give yourself up in truth and sincerity to this spirit of prayer, I will venture to affirm that, if you had twice as many evil spirits in you as Mary Magdalene had, they will all be cast out of you, and you will be forced with her to weep tears of love at the feet of the holy Jesus.

I knew I was proud. It was something I recognized and prayed to God often to help me change. But I didn't know the depth or the seriousness of my sin.

For two weeks I prayed the prayer above, earnestly seeking God to show me how He saw me. For those two weeks I didn't sense anything differently to speak of. I remember actually thinking to myself, maybe I'm not so proud after all. Until one Sunday, God in His kindness opened the floodgates of conviction. It started with me simply asking Tom to do something during our Sunday service. He was in the middle of praying for someone and I interrupted him to tell him what I was thinking. Afterward as we were driving home he mentioned to me the awkwardness of my interrupting him. I would like to say I listened to him and apologized. But I didn't. I got angry; steaming angry.

Tom got out to pump gas in our car, but the fumes inside our car were more noxious. As I was mulling over what he said – the Lord quickened to my heart this thought:

This is pride. I want you to repent to Tom for the way you're acting. I am answering your prayer.

Those words were few, but sharper than a two-edged sword. My conscience was pierced and the tears began to flow. By the time Tom got in the car he had no clue as to what was wrong. I couldn't talk. I was convicted in a way I've never felt conviction before. This was an experience my pride had never allowed.

For the next few weeks every where I looked in my life I saw pride. It was there behind every motive, every phone conversation, every thought and every deed. God literally opened the flood gates and had it not been for the depth of His grace and His loving hand to stop when I could bear no more, I wouldn't have endured.

Following this experience, I realized something. Tom now knew the ugly side of my heart. The part I had worked so hard to hide from others. The funny thing is as I repented to others, my pride wasn't a surprise to them at all. They saw it, but loved me anyway. Wow!

Maybe God is wanting you to pursue an honesty which breeds intimacy with God – with your spouse? But be forewarned; it can be ugly at first.

God has promised He will never leave you or forsake you. He will walk this road with you and help you say NO to ungodliness in whatever form this has taken in your heart and marriage. The purpose is to have a marriage built upon the solid rock of Christ. All other foundations must crumble in order to build a loving relationship which will endure any storm. It is all for Him and His glory that we do these things.

I promise, if you ask God to show you how to do this, He will be faithful to show you.

JANUARY

1. *"It is more blessed to GIVE than to RECEIVE."*

2. Take every opportunity to celebrate your spouse's victories - the small ones, and the big ones. *"Rejoice with those who rejoice!"*

3. Every now and then, do an unexpected kindness for your spouse. Last night I received a neck and shoulder massage while watching TV. Amazing how such kindness builds gratefulness.

4. We're all just a phone call away from life-changing news. Be grateful today for the routine, ready for the interruptions, constant in prayer, and full of faith in the God who orchestrates it all!

5. Be willing to endure the difficulties with your spouse, side by side, each lending support where needed.

6. Loyalty and disloyalty in marriage express themselves through our conversation with others. One builds up - the other tears down. Work on building today!

7. Romance isn't about proving anything; It's about expressing something.

8. Know what your spouse is wishing for. How can you help make it happen?

9. Outdo one another in showing honor!

10. Never compare your spouse or your marriage to others. This makes us either puffed up thinking ours is better - or discontent thinking ours isn't good enough.

11. NEVER use absolutes when it comes to resolving conflicts. But ALWAYS use them to express your love and commitment!

12. A triple braided cord is not easily broken. (paraphrased from the Bible). Remember the strength of a strong marriage is not in our love for each other, but in His love for US!

13. *"A soft answer turns away wrath, but a harsh word stirs up anger."* Proverbs 15:1 ESV

14. Is there something your spouse has asked you to do and you've been putting it off? Why not do it today? This is expressing your love for them in word AND deed!

15. Do something unexpected and kind for your spouse today!

16. Study your spouse well so your marriage will pass the test of time.

17. Recapture the lazy, Sunday afternoon tradition with your spouse by making plans to take a nap together this Sunday.

18. *"If you don't know where you're going, you'll get there every time."* - Yogi Berra. Where do you want your marriage to be 5 or 10 years from now?

19. Find a way to communicate to your spouse, even across a crowded room, your desire for them alone!

20. *"Don't find fault. Find a remedy; anybody can complain."* — Henry Ford

21. Express gratefulness today for the way your spouse sacrifices for you. Hint: It may be the small things you currently take for granted.

22. When going away together - turn your spouse on and social media off!

23. *"Write your injuries in dust, your benefits in marble."* - Benjamin Franklin

24. *"Be kind to one another, tenderhearted, forgiving one another, as God in Christ forgave you."* Ephesians 4:32 ESV

25. In case you're wondering...Yes, it's worth it!!

26. Remember those things that attracted you to your spouse when you first met. Doing this keeps the home fires burning!

27. Every day we make choices to build up or tear down. How are you building your marriage this day?

28. Be sure to sympathize with your spouse in their weaknesses - this not only glorifies God; but it strengthens your marriage as well!

29. Send encouraging words to your spouse via e-mail or text. Nothing brightens a ho-hum day like a surprise "smile" in your inbox!

30. Keep a short list of offenses. The longer we hold them the more embittered we become. *"Love keeps no record of wrongs..."*

January Cultivation Questions
Our Endurance

1. What does it mean to endure suffering in regard to your marriage?

2. If you aren't suffering now, what can you do to prepare for the time when you will?

3. Considering the suffering Christ endured for us on the Cross; how can this fact help you face difficulties?

4. If marriage is more about "our holiness than our happiness" as John Piper states, how can this help us walk through seasons of suffering together?

Date Night Prompt
Celebrate The Five Senses

With all this talk about suffering, how appropriate to administer peace and relaxation to our spouse. Make your bedroom into an At Home Spa Retreat. Celebrate all the senses together:

Five Senses: Spend one evening celebrating the senses of your relationship:

Seeing: Look at pictures from when you first fell in love. Look at current pictures and marvel at how you've changed, grown and fallen more in love than you imagined possible.

Hearing: Listen to your favorite romantic song together while looking in each other's eyes. Let the words of the song communicate your heart and love.

Smelling: Light an aromatic candle and enjoy a hot bubble bath together.

Tasting: Chocolate is a known aphrodisiac. How about some delicious fondue? No fondue forks? No problem...feed your spouse with your fingers.

Touching: Back massage, foot and leg massage – you name the body part – the touching is the best sense when it comes to being romantic.

From The Romantic Vineyard Blog

Love Endures All Things

Date night – 1982.

Tom took me to the theater to see a new movie that was receiving rave reviews. It was Monday; we had both worked all day; I was 7 months pregnant with our first child, but we couldn't wait. We made sure no one told us about the movie so as not to spoil it.

We wished someone had!

You see the movie we're talking about had a name that was powerful and sounded like another action-packed, heart pounding movie we had recently seen and loved – *Raiders of the Lost Ark.*

This movie was nothing like it.

The title *Chariots of Fire* was deceiving in that there were no grand chariot races, no overcoming great obstacles – at least not the obvious kinds we had imagined. This race was of another sort – the race of one's personal best and willingness to endure.

We're sad to say, we weren't up to such deep thinking that night. In fact, I fell asleep! We were amazed when the movie continued to do well in the box office. When it ended up winning the Academy Award for Best Movie – we were shocked. I remember asking, "Did we miss something?"

Apparently, we had! Actually, the whole point of Eric Liddell's amazing testimony. What does this have to do with marriage? Everything.

In the next part of 1 Corinthians 13:4-7 it says, *"Love endures ALL things."* This endurance can be related to a runner in a race. We all run in one way or another – but are we willing to endure? To move past the obstacles in the road and run with our whole heart until the end?

Half of all marriages in America end in divorce. They fail in this important aspect of love – to endure ALL things. We have had our share of enduring hardship: a miscarriage, two back surgeries, loss of jobs, barely enough money to pay the bills, death of loved ones, confession of secret sins, forgiveness of those sins, national crisis as well as personal crisis. We have learned how to wait patiently for answers we had no certainty would ever come. We have learned in the waiting that God is faithful. We have grown in our ability to listen because we have endured conversation that wasn't fun. There has been much endurance, and after all these years we see the benefit.

When a runner first begins training just making it the first mile can be torture. But as he continues training something happens – the muscles and heart begin to work together finding a rhythm that brings a steady pace. Ground is gained and with it the freedom to run full speed ahead. This is the moment when records are broken. When a runner reaches this place there is joy in the running no matter how painful it may be.

Eric Liddell said, *"I believe God made me for a purpose, but he also made me fast. And when I run I feel His pleasure."*

In the same way, God made us husband and wife for a purpose. He has given us all we need to grow in godliness and the ability to endure. When we do, we feel His pleasure and this makes it all worth it.

In what ways are you having to endure?

FEBRUARY

1. Oftentimes we don't appreciate something until it's gone. In what ways do you appreciate your spouse?

2. Marriage is a glorious opportunity to die to self and grow in esteeming others as more important than yourself! What is your focus - dying or growing?

3. *"Pursue peace with all men"* - especially spouses. Pursue means to try to find, get, win; strive for; seek after PEACE.

4. Keep a short list of grievances, or they will quickly become a long list of bitterness!

5. The only way to truly love others [your spouse] is by loving God!

6. Never take for granted the privilege it is to worship God together.

7. A godly marriage allows others to see-through them to see the beauty of Christ's love for His church on display, and it is glorious.

8. Give thanks each day this week for the godly attributes your spouse displays on a regular basis.

9. Come, let me love you in the years to come as I have in the years gone by.

10. Welcoming the input of Godly counsel into your marriage will open the door to a deeper, more satisfying love.

11. Building a good marriage is a lot like building a house in an earthquake zone–if you find a fault, don't build on it.

12. Romantic moments can be as simple as pausing to marvel at God's creation together.

13. Express your love in ordinary ways every day but do it in an extraordinary way today to create a romantic memory for your spouse to cherish.

14. Celebrate Valentine's Day every day, in the way you think of and treat your spouse!

15. Healthy communication is a married couples' greatest weapon. Use it often and watch your relationship grow.

16. Boredom in marriage can reveal an area of needed change. Only those who are willing to face it instead of run will benefit from it.

17. It's the little things you do or don't do that have the biggest impact on your marriage.

18. Vowing to love each other when facing times where neither likes each other or the circumstances you're facing so much is evidence of God's grace and the certainty you'll make it through.

19. Be grateful for the way your spouse demonstrates God's love in the way he/she loves you.

20. Be sure your spouse knows this fact: Yours is the hand I reach for when I need comfort, help, and support.

21. Reserve space in your heart and your marriage for God. When we expect His arrival, He always shows up.

22. Intimacy deepens when we choose to be quiet together. This works spiritually, emotionally and physically.

23. Marriage is made up of two people who are growing in their relationship with Christ. The more we grow personally in our relationship with Him, the better our marriage will be.

24. Be sure your spouse knows you love them even if you are facing a boring season in your marriage. Keeping your heart open to God in the boredom will guarantee it's passing if you listen and respond.

25. Abiding in the vine of Christ provides the grace and support your marriage needs to produce quality fruit that remains.

26. New mercies which dawn each morning provide the help and hope your marriage needs today.

27. Take time to consider how far you've come since you both said, "I do." This will give you needed perspective and hope for the road ahead.

28. Don't underestimate the power of a good question asked at the right time to take your communication to a deeper level.

29. Be sure to resolve the seemingly "little" conflicts. To ignore them is to allow them to continue to gnaw at the root of your marriage causing more damage.

February Cultivation Questions
Our Love Never Fails

1. In what ways are you pursuing a deeper relationship with God? Making Him the priority is the best way to increase love for your spouse.

2. Share with your spouse the ways they demonstrate God's love by the way they love you. Be specific.

3. If love never fails, why is it important to pursue love above all else in our marriage?

4. What characteristic do you love and appreciate the most in your spouse? Tell them.

Date Night Prompt
Home Fires Burning

Plan a date around a fire

If you have a fireplace, enjoy a cozy night together.

If you have a fire pit outside, roast marshmallows and relax.

If you don't have either of these, light lots of candles and turn off all the lights. Let the glow of the flickering flames set the stage for intimacy.

From The Romantic Vineyard Blog

Paul sums it all up by declaring, "*Love never fails!*"
Wow! How many marriages would endure if both the husband and wife had this conviction of heart. If something isn't able to fail, then whatever happens must be endured. And not only endured but worked on to improve and strengthen.

The love Paul has outlined for us is impossible left to ourselves. We are incapable of loving our spouse the way God intended. Only Adam and Eve experienced this kind of marital bliss, yet even they weren't satisfied. They had perfection, but desired still more!

If Adam and Eve weren't content, how is it possible for us to cling to such commitment? Only by allowing God to love our spouse through us. As we have each received perfect love from the Lord which will never fail; we can trust in the same way He will allow us to love others, our spouse included, far above what we ever thought was possible. It is a miracle, and one which brings great glory to Him.

If our love doesn't fail, it is only by His grace at work within us. Every year as you celebrate your anniversary, remember "*It is God who works in you, both to will and to work for His good pleasure.*" Philippians 2:13.

Now for a quick recap of what we've discovered about love as defined in the 1 Corinthians 13.

Love is patient – The Holy Spirit who is perfectly patient with us helps us in our weakness to grow so our marriages become a reflection of Him!

Love is kind – True kindness takes no regard for how it is received; for kindness that is real flows from a heart that longs to please God, not man. It has no strings attached.

Love does not envy – If I am allowing myself to think envious thoughts, I am NOT loving my husband/wife. See it. Admit it. Confess it. Repent of it. And be free from it! We don't have to live this way. Christ has set us free from the bonds of slavery to sin; this includes envy.

Love does not boast – Boasting is a manifestation of pride, and pride concerns itself with self – not others. We can't truly love our spouse if we are boasting in ourselves and what we've done or plan to do. We must look out for the interests of our spouse – what pleases them, what would serve them.

Love is not rude – Rude behavior is the outflow of a selfish heart.

Love is not arrogant – Arrogance and humility are both undetected by its possessors. The proof comes from the observations of those who are closest to us. Only the humble person will ask!

Love does not insist on its own way – I must not insist on my own way, but I must also embrace the way of another. This can be my spouse's way, God's way, or someone else's way (like cranky babies, unruly toddlers, or rebellious teens). Love demands that I set aside my own agenda to serve another.

Love is not irritable – God has provided much for me – more than I deserve. He has done for me that which I could never do for myself – made peace between Him and me. I will never understand such kindness, such mercy. As I meditate on this Truth I can feel my irritations taking a back seat to gratefulness.

Love is not resentful – When we choose to love each other the way God ordains, suddenly what mattered before doesn't matter anymore. We realize we aren't loving, and it's easier to let go. If love is NOT resentful, and if love is NOT a feeling, but a choice we make, then we can choose to change with God's help.

Love does not rejoice in wrong-doing but rejoices in the truth – We can easily look at this portion of 1 Corinthians 13 and assume we never rejoice in wrong doing. But we must take a closer look–dig deeper than the surface. We tend to gloss over things rather than mulling them over and inquiring of God for His help to accurately assess our hearts and what motivates us.

Love bears all things – True love is willing to bear the little things, the big things, the inconvenient things and the unexpected things. True love bears ALL things – after all, this is what Christ has done for us. He gave us the most He possibly could – Himself!

Love believes all things – We live in a society that thrives on being critical of everyone! Let's go against the flow by choosing to believe the best instead of looking for the worst. It's a much more loving way to live – and it glorifies God!

Love hopes all things – We all have areas where change hasn't happened or any progress we have made is too small to notice. Yet God has promised to complete the work He's begun in us. This applies to our spouse as well! Don't give up hope! As long as we are living and breathing there is always hope for change.

Love endures all things – God made us husband and wife for a purpose. He has given us all we need to grow in godliness and the ability to endure. When we do we feel His pleasure and He is glorified.

Love never fails!

"Catch the foxes for us..."

Marriage is a privilege, a gift from God that allows us to reflect the love Christ has for the church.

In our culture often the most important part of getting married is the wedding! Imagine if a vineyard owner did the same. Spending his time, attention and money on a vineyard, only to neglect them after they're in the ground. How foolish.

Yet many marriages give more thought to the wedding than they do to the marriage.

In Song of Solomon it says:
"Catch the foxes for us,
the little foxes
that spoil the vineyards,
for our vineyards are in blossom."
(Song of Solomon 2:15 ESV)

A fox doesn't come and only eat the fruit of the vine–they do much more damage. They like to gnaw on the trunk, dig holes around it and expose the roots. They like to destroy the entire vine!

So the question begs itself: What foxes are chewing on your marriage vine?

Fox #1: Unresolved conflict – this includes unforgiveness.

Fox #2: Uncharitable judgments – not thinking the best,
but assuming the worst.

Fox #3: Neglect

Fox #4: All work and no play

Fox #5: Idols of the heart – video games, shopping, children,
addicted to work, selfishness, pleasure, etc.

Fox #6: Lack of purpose

All the above can cause lasting damage to the marriage if they aren't caught and dealt with quickly. So how do we trap these little foxes? How do we recognize them in our own marriage?

We have found that the best way to assess the health of our marriage is to examine how we are relating to each other.

- If there is tension, then there may be a fox of unresolved conflict lurking around.

- If you tend to judge your spouse's motives, there may be a fox of unforgiveness chewing at your heart.

- If you have not had regular time alone together, then you should look more closely for the fox of neglect.

- Perhaps you find your mind constantly at work, even when you're "off". Or you don't look at them when they speak, and you only listen to them halfway. This could be the fox of all work and no play.

- The fox of idols of the heart can be much more difficult to catch. This is because our idols are the things that have not only caught our attention, but our affection. To discover them we must examine where our thoughts go when we have nothing else to think about? Or what do I want to do more than anything else with my free time? Just because we desire to do something doesn't mean it is an idol, but it could be. The only way to know for sure is to ask God to help you discover this little fox. He will be faithful to help you see it.

- The last fox is lack of purpose. He loves to get us to fall asleep in the vineyard, so he can work his damage on the vine. This is why Date Nights are so important. It encourages us to be intentional in pursuing our spouse.

What foxes have you discovered today prowling about your marriage vineyard? We encourage you to do the work necessary to chase them away. If you do, the fruit produced in your vineyard will be good and satisfying.

A successful marriage requires falling in love many times, always with the same person. – Mignon McLaughlin